First published in 2010 by Wayland
Text copyright © Pat Thomas 2010
Illustrations copyright © Lesley Harker 2010

Wayland
Hachette Children's Books
338, Euston Road,
London NW1 3BH

Wayland Australia
Level 17/207 Kent Street
Sydney, NSW 2000

Concept design: Kate Buxton
Title design: D-R-ink

British Library Cataloguing in Publication Data
Thomas, Pat, 1959-
I can make a difference : a first look at setting a good
example. -- (A first look at)
1. Conduct of life--Juvenile literature. 2. Influence
(Psychology)--Juvenile literature.
I. Title II. Series
158-dc22

ISBN: 978 0 7502 6138 8

Printed in China

Wayland is a division of Hachette Children's Books,
an Hachette UK company.
www.hachette.co.uk

I Can Make a Difference

A FIRST LOOK AT SETTING A GOOD EXAMPLE

PAT THOMAS

ILLUSTRATED BY LESLEY HARKER

Every person in the world is a teacher.
Even you. Did you know that?

Every day we teach each other
how to do things. And we learn
from each other too – even if
we don't always know it.

When we watch someone, and copy the things they do,
we are learning from their example.

If we copy people who set a good example,
by behaving well and treating others with kindness,
that is how we will learn to behave.

And if we copy people who
behave badly, and treat others unkindly,
that is how we will learn to behave, too.

The best way to set a good example is to treat others the way you want them to treat you...

...and to take care of your family, your friends and
your home in the way you would like others to
take care of them.

Some people set good examples for us all in the work that they do.

But all of us can find ways to set
a good example every day.

13

You can set a good example by saying 'please' and 'thank you', never calling names and offering to help...

... or by protecting those who are smaller or weaker than you, and helping to keep things clean and tidy.

You can help by carrying the heavy things,
not throwing rubbish on the ground, congratulating
the winning team, or reading to a sick friend.

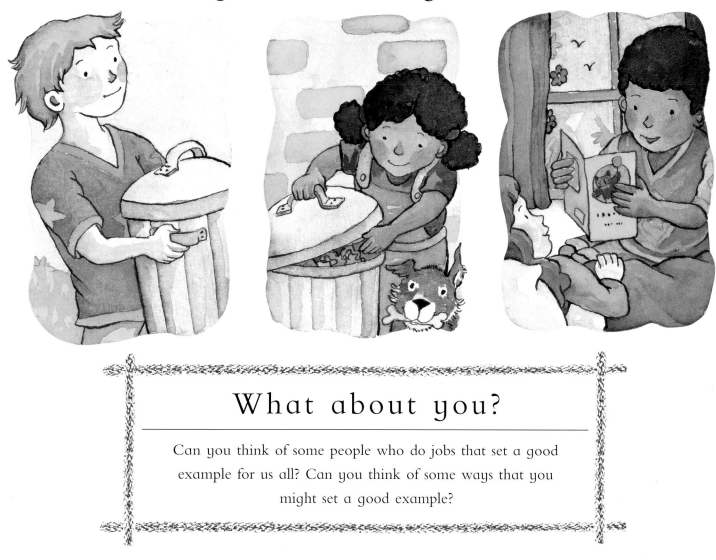

What about you?

Can you think of some people who do jobs that set a good
example for us all? Can you think of some ways that you
might set a good example?

It's not just about taking care
of others, though.

You can also set
a good example by
taking good care of yourself.

Nobody's perfect all the time.

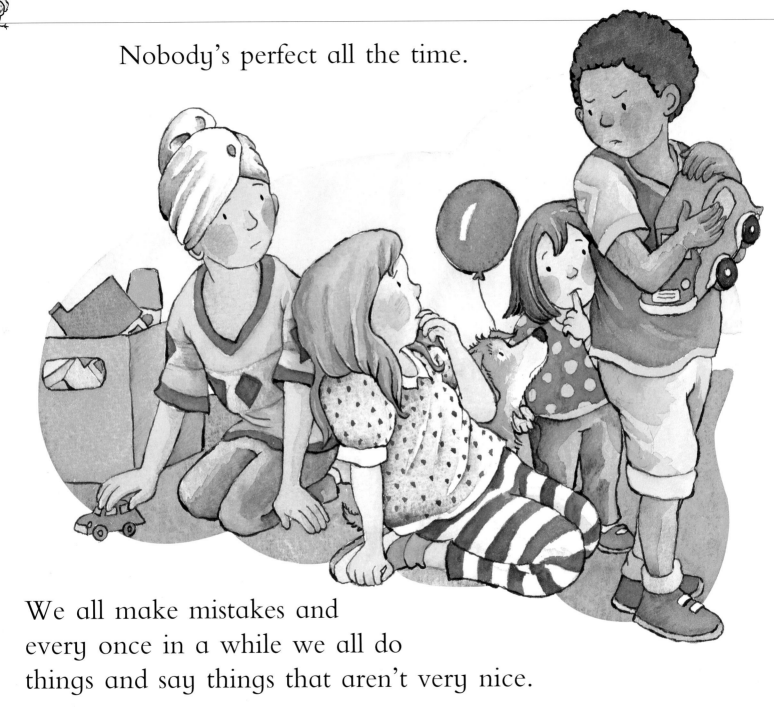

We all make mistakes and
every once in a while we all do
things and say things that aren't very nice.

When that happens saying
'I'm sorry' – and meaning it –
is another way to set
a good example.

Sometimes you might wonder why
it is important to set a good example.
Especially when you see other
people who never do.

You might also wonder if the way one person acts can really make a difference. Lots of adults wonder this too.

What about you?

Can you think of some times when you have seen other people setting a poor example? What happened? How did that make you feel?

Every person on earth has a choice about how they behave and how they treat others.

By setting a good example, and doing your best, you are teaching other people to act the same way.

And if those people copy you, then everyone they know will also learn this important lesson.

When everyone tries their best to behave well, it makes our families, our classrooms and our communities nicer places to be.

It makes working and playing together easier
and more enjoyable.

Most people who choose to be kind and polite to others want to make the world a better place.

It's like planting seeds in a garden.
The more you plant, the more beautiful
the garden will become.

HOW TO USE THIS BOOK

It has been said that there are only three things a parent needs to know about raising considerate, responsible, well mannered children: Example, example, example. Who children become is deeply influenced by the example set by those who raise them. So, as a first step, it's worth considering what kind of example we want to set, what qualities we would like our children to have when they grow up, and examining how we as parents and caregivers can communicate these values.

Simple good examples any parent or caregiver can set involve: using kind words, helping when you can, sharing, listening to what others have to say, being honest and truthful, thinking before you speak and act, practising good manners, controlling your temper, thinking about the feelings of others, and applying the principles of fairness at home and at work.

In addition, provide context where you can – about why showing kindness and consideration for others is important and how it can have a positive 'knock on' effect in the wider world. Children often have no idea why we do what we do, so talk about what you are doing and why. If we take soup to a sick friend, or if we work on a community project, explain why you think it's important to be helpful and/or take some responsibility in the community. This can help our children understand our reasoning and relate our activities to their own behaviour.

Try taking a step-by-step approach. Start with the 'magic words' such as "please" and "thank you". Gradually add more examples such as "you're welcome" and "pardon me?" and "may I…". As children get a little older, you can work on actions like picking up toys, table manners, looking after siblings, taking care of pets, etc.

Remember to compliment your children when they behave well. Saying "Holding the door for that woman carrying all those heavy bags was very polite." "I saw how well you got on with everyone at sports day. Well done." will send a more positive message than constantly reprimanding them when they are not behaving well.

Young children are old enough to understand rules and the consequences of breaking those rules. When defining what is and isn't acceptable behaviour, parents and teachers alike can help by setting fair rules with clear explanations for why these have been set.

You can't always get it right. We all lose our tempers, say things we're sorry for, or are not always as kind as we would like to be. Admit your failures, apologise where you need to, and move on with a view to how you might act differently next time. Remember, you are aiming to provide a solid framework of values - for your child to live up to, but which the whole family can live within.

Schools provide ample opportunities for children to practice a whole range of social skills and many of the lessons about setting a good example can be found in general citizenship lessons. Visits from people in the community who are helping others, such as community nurses, police officers, firemen, religious leaders and environmentalists, are a good time to initiate discussions about working with others, caring for ourselves and the wider community, and behaving responsibly. Children can be encouraged to ask questions, take photos and perhaps make a book and/or poster about such visits.

Giving children jobs in the classroom or the school, for example, making class drinks, delivering post, taking care of animals, assisting children with learning or physical disabilities, enhances a sense of responsibility and engagement.

BOOKS TO READ

Teaching Citizenship Through Traditional Tales
Sue Ellis, Deirdre Grogan (Scholastic, 2003)

I'll Do It!: Learning About Responsibility
Brian Moses (Wayland, 1998)

The Bad Good Manners Book
Babette Cole (Hamish Hamilton Ltd, 1995)

Why Should I Share?
Claire Llewellyn (Wayland, 2002)

Why Should I Recycle?
Jen Green (Wayland, 2002)

RESOURCES FOR ADULTS

How to Talk So Kids Will Listen and Listen So Kids Will Talk (How to Help Your Child)
Adele Faber, Elain Mazlish (Piccadilly Press Ltd, 2001)

Teaching Your Children Values
Lind and Richard Eyre (Fireside, 1993)